# Contents

Jimmy Rabbit's Adventure

Jimmy rabbit was born on a warm evening in May 2009 in England. Celebrations had been going on in the town set back in the distant hills. Jimmy's mother had been very frightened by all the noisy fireworks going off into the night. All she could hear whilst snuggled up in her warm burrow were high pitched gushing noises followed by enormous bangs and then a flash would literally light up her home.

She had been very busy preparing her nest ready for her new arrivals that were safe and snug inside her womb unaware of their surroundings.

Four sleepy days later Mummy rabbit finally gave birth to her two twin rabbits. She called them Jimmy and Josie. They were such beautiful little rabbits and looked like balls of white fluff with enormous eyes! Jimmy had blue eyes and Josie's were brown.

They snuggled close to their mother for warmth and slept for many days, only waking to feed from their mother who never left their side. These two tiny balls of fluff soon grew larger and became very inquisitive about what was at the end of the tunnel to their cosy home.

Finally the warmth from the sun shone down into their burrow and Jimmy and Josie finally hopped with excitement from the safety of their home out into the big wide world. Mummy rabbit kept a very close eye on them both as she was very aware of the dangers that lurked beyond their burrow.

Jimmy and Josie's tiny little noses twitched as they could smell the fresh spring air. The green meadow shimmered in the sunlight and the long grass

swayed in the breeze.  They could hear the birds singing in

the trees and every now and then a butterfly or a bee would hover above them.        Mummy        rabbit

made them sit quite still and asked them to listen seriously to her. She told them that they had to be vey careful not to wander too far away because there were many dangerous predators out there beyond the meadow. She knew they were excited to go and explore and needed to practice their bunny hops, so she finally told them that they could circle the meadow just the once and return straight back to her.

At this Jimmy and Josie were off like a shot, hopping at great speed through the grass. Jimmy was much faster than Josie and got way ahead in no time! Jimmy shouted to Josie "I am going to find a hiding place and you must come and find me". Jimmy could see in the distance a little hill with hole in it just like his home. He scampered up to it and then decided to go down into the tunnel out of sight of Josie.

It was much steeper than he thought and he suddenly found himself rolling over and over until something hard stopped his fall. It was a little wooden door! It had a metal knocker on it so curious Jimmy knocked three times with a rat-a-tat-tat! Suddenly, to his amazement, the door opened and he could not believe his eyes!

There before him was this beautiful garden full of brightly coloured creatures and flowers! He hopped into the garden and completely forgot about his poor sister Josie and her mummy who were still in the meadow somewhere above the tunnel.

His eyes widened as he took in the sights. There were butterflies, ladybirds, caterpillars, spiders, grasshoppers, crickets, dragonflies, all going about their business, some munching on leaves, others flitting from one flower to another.

Suddenly, a red and yellow snail approached him very slowly and said in a very gentle voice "hello little rabbit, what are you doing here"? At this

Jimmy rabbit replied "Oh, I am hiding from my sister and

she will never find me here, wherever here is.  Can you please tell me where we are Mr Snail"?

The snail smiled at Jimmy and said "Why this is Jeramiah's

Garden little rabbit and you are very safe here".    Jimmy breathed a sigh of relief and continued to say to the snail "It is so beautiful and peaceful here, I like it and everyone is so friendly".    Just then Jimmy's tummy gave a rumble and so he said to the snail "Can I possibly have something to eat from your garden"?.

The snail quickly pointed to row upon row of large juicy carrots and lettuces and said "The farmer will not mind you helping yourself little rabbit, go ahead and eat as much as you want".

Jimmy replied "What is a farmer"? and the snail replied "A farmer is a human man who looks after Jeramiah's Garden and makes sure that there is always enough for everyone to eat, including us creatures and animals".

Jimmy heard a strange noise and he looked through the wooden fence and saw the farmer on a strange machine out in the fields.  He gasped "What is that"?

The snail replied "That is the farmer's tractor which digs the field so that the farmer can sow his corn and once it grows then another machine collects the corn once it reaches the right height.  The farmer then grinds the corn into flour to make bread, cereals and cakes for his family to eat and he also collects hay for his animals to eat".

Jimmy was amazed to hear this and he thought to himself ......this human must be a very special man to provide such a beautiful garden for all these creatures and grow food to feed everybody.

He immediately felt very happy and relaxed and began munching on the delicious carrots and lettuce until he was absolutely full to the brim!

Suddenly he remembered his sister Josie and her mother whom he had left in the meadow and quickly said to the snail "Oh no.....I must go back to the meadow to find my family before they worry about me". The snail said to Jimmy "Go little rabbit and find your family and bring them back to Jeramiah's Garden so that you can all live in safety and will never have to worry about having to face the predators that lurk up there.

You will all have plenty to eat here and the sun shines every day". At this Jimmy rabbit ran back through the doorway and hopped very fast up the tunnel. On his way up he saw a large worm, a centipede and a blue and green beetle. They said to Jimmy "Where does this lead to little rabbit"? Jimmy replied "Keep going until you come to the little wooden door, knock three times and you will be invited into Jeramiah's Garden where you can eat all you want and sleep in safety"! The worm said "Why thank you little rabbit, we will be on our way".

Jimmy continued hopping up the tunnel until he came back out into the meadow. He could hear his mother and sister calling him very loudly so he ran very fast out into the open and shouted back "I am here and I have a lovely surprise for you both".

Mummy rabbit was so relieved to see Jimmy but at the same time gave him a scolding and told him off for running away. "Wherever have you been Jimmy? Did I not tell you never to go out of my sight? I have been very worried about you and so was your sister."

Jimmy was still very excited about his adventure and said very loudly "I have found Jeramiah's Garden and we must go there right away"! Mummy rabbit refused to listen to Jimmy and grabbed him by the fur and said angrily "I am taking you back to our burrow and I am going to ground you          for          a          whole          week

for running off and not listening to me". Jimmy was still

trying to tell his mother about his adventure but mummy
rabbit was not listening to Jimmy

and took him back to his home. Jimmy cried for days and felt very sad that his mother would not listen to him. Jimmy dreamt about the garden at night

and in the mornings his wonderful dreams kept him going
all day.  Five days passed and all was very quiet in the

meadow above until one dark night the sound of dogs barking and shotguns being fired woke the family of rabbits. Mother rabbit ran to the top of the tunnel to see what was happening closely followed by Jimmy and Josie.

Mother rabbit's heart sank and she started to tremble with fear. "Oh no" she cried......."It's the hunters with their dogs, they will find us for sure and kill us!" Jimmy thought quickly and said to his mother "We have time to run to Jeramiah's Garden and we will be safe there.......follow me".

At this Jimmy scampered off into the meadow closely followed by his mother and Josie. They all ran as fast as their little legs would go and the hunter's dogs spotted them! "Don't stop mother and Josie, keep up with me, we can make it, I know we can" shouted Jimmy!

The dogs got closer and closer but Jimmy found the tunnel and dived in with his mother and Josie right behind him!..........down they slid until they reached the wooden door.

This time the door was already open and the snail was waiting for them. As soon as they were all through the door, the snail slammed it shut with an almighty bang!

They could hear the dogs on the other side of the door barking ferociously. Mr snail said "do not worry they cannot get through the door, it is safely locked! Mother rabbit was crying and shaking and poor Josie was terribly out of breath! The snail said to Mummy rabbit "Fear not Mrs Rabbit for you and your family are now safe in Jeramiah's wonderful garden where you can stay forever and live in peace and harmony with God's creatures and beautiful

nature and have all the food you will ever need"! Mummy

rabbit stopped crying and looked around her in amazement! She put her arms around Jimmy

and said "Jimmy I am so sorry my child for not listening to you before.  You have surely saved our lives today and I will never forget that. At least now we can enjoy the sunshine without living in fear and you will be able to grow up and raise a family of your own and I will be able to enjoy my grandchildren with the knowledge that we are in Jeramiah's wonderful garden, safe from danger.

Jimmy was so happy and relieved that he and his family were now safe.

They remained in Jeramiah's Garden for the rest of their lives and lived happily ever after!

THE END

www.ingramcontent.com/pod-product-compliance
Lightning Source LLC
Chambersburg PA
CBHW060816290526
45792CB00005BB/1677

*9 7 8 1 4 9 7 5 8 0 6 4 0 *